Kangaroos

Kangaroos

A Carolrhoda Nature Watch Book

by Denise Burt
photographs by Neil McLeod
edited by Sylvia A. Johnson

Carolrhoda Books, Inc. / Minneapolis

Additional photographs courtesy of: © Jean-Paul Ferrero/
AUSCAPE, pp.4–5, 6, 19, 44; © Werner Forman/Art
Resources, NY, p. 38.

Carolrhoda Books, Inc.
A division of Lerner Publishing Group
241 First Avenue North, Minneapolis, MN 55401 U.S.A.

Website address: www.lernerbooks.com

Library of Congress Cataloging-in-Publication Data

Burt, Denise.
    Kangaroos / by Denise Burt ; photographs by Neil
McLeod ; edited by Sylvia A. Johnson.
        p. cm.
    Summary: Describes the physical characteristics, diet,
behavior, and life cycle of kangaroos, as well as their
relationship with humans.
    ISBN 1-57505-388-8 (lib. bdg. : alk. paper)
    1. Kangaroos—Juvenile literature. [1. Kangaroos.]
I. McLeod, Neil, ill. II. Johnson, Sylvia A. III. Title
QL737.M35B87   2000
599.2'22—dc21   99-26680

Manufactured in the United States of America
2 3 4 5 6 7 – JR – 06 05 04 03 02 01

CONTENTS

WHAT IS A KANGAROO?

Everyone knows what a kangaroo is. It's a large animal with big ears, short reddish-colored fur, powerful hind legs, and a long, heavy tail. It lives in Australia, where it can be found hopping around on the open plains eating grass.

This is a pretty good description of one kangaroo. But would it surprise you to find out that there are more than 50 kinds of animals called kangaroos? And that some of them are as different from this big grass-eating variety as a beagle is from a Saint Bernard?

In this book, you will meet a few of the fascinating animals called kangaroos.

Kangaroos (left) *and koalas* (right) *belong to the scientific order of marsupials. Like all their relatives, they produce young that go through most of their development in pouches.*

KANGAROOS LARGE AND SMALL

Talking about kangaroos can be confusing. These animals have many names, and sometimes the same name can mean different things to different people. Let's try to come up with some useful terms.

When scientists discuss kangaroos, one term they always use is **marsupial** (mar-SOO-pee-uhl). Kangaroos belong to a scientific **order,** or group, called Marsupialia. This order is made up of animals that produce their young in a special way.

A baby marsupial is born in a very early stage of development. It continues its growth in a pouch located on the outside of its mother's body. Because marsupials are **mammals,** just as humans are, the baby is nourished by its mother's milk.

Within the marsupial order, there are 18 smaller groups called **families.** The opossums that live in North and South America belong to one family. All other marsupials are found in and around Australia. Koalas make up one family of Australian marsupials, and wombats another.

Two families of marsupials include animals usually called kangaroos. One is made up of **potoroids** (POH-tuh-royds), or rat kangaroos. The other, much larger family consists of **macropods** (MAK-roh-pods). This word means "big foot" and refers to one of the main features of most kangaroos. The macropod family includes more than 50 individual species, or kinds, of kangaroos.

Red kangaroos are the largest members of the macropod family, with males weighing as much as 200 pounds (about 90 kg). Standing on its hind legs, a big red male (below) can measure more than 6 feet tall (almost 2 m). Females weigh about half as much as males, and their fur is usually a smoky gray color. Grass eaters that live in dry open country, red kangaroos are the animals most non-Australians think of when they hear the word "kangaroo."

Left: This little creature is a potoroo (POH-tuh-roo), one of the potoroid, or rat, kangaroos. Like most members of this family, it is not much bigger than a rat. Potoroos make nests out of plant material, carrying leaves and grass in their curled-up tails. They sleep in their nests during the day, going out at night to find food. Their diet includes insects as well as plant roots and seeds.

Right: Wallabies belong to the macropod family. There are about 27 species of these marsupials, ranging from hare wallabies about the size of large rabbits to animals weighing as much as 60 pounds (about 27 kg). Shown here is a young swamp wallaby, one of the medium-sized members of the group. Swamp wallabies live in eastern Australia, inhabiting dry areas as well as wet, swampy ones. Their diet includes a wide variety of plants.

Left: Pademelons are small macropods weighing no more than 15 pounds (about 7 kg). Their name, like those of many other marsupials, comes from a language spoken by the Aborigines, the native people of Australia. These small kangaroos live in forests in eastern Australia and on the island of New Guinea. They eat grass, roots, and small plants.

A female western gray kangaroo with a baby in her pouch. This macropod species and the closely related eastern gray kangaroo are large animals, with males weighing as much as 145 pounds (about 66 kg). "Gray" kangaroos have soft fur that is often gray brown in color. They live in wooded areas and eat grass.

Right: Nailtail wallabies got their name because they have small, horny spurs at the ends of their tails, something like human fingernails. The picture shows a bridled nailtail wallaby, which has markings that look like a horse's bridle on its shoulders and neck. This small wallaby (weighing an average of 14 pounds—about 6 kg) was thought to be extinct but was rediscovered in the 1970s. The area where bridled nailtails live has become a nature refuge.

Left: This slender, graceful animal is a wallaroo, a member of the macropod family. Its name, a combination of "wallaby" and "kangaroo," refers to its size—larger than most wallabies but smaller than giant macropods such as the red kangaroo. Scientists have identified at least two species of wallaroos. Shown here is the antilopine wallaroo, which is common in warm, tropical areas of northern Australia. Like the antelopes of Africa, antilopines feed mainly on grass. They are fairly large animals, the males weighing as much as 110 pounds (about 50 kg).

BIG FEET MADE FOR HOPPING

Large or small, forest dwellers or inhabitants of the plains, most kangaroos have one thing in common. Their preferred method of travel is hopping.

Kangaroos have four legs, but they are built very differently than deer and other four-legged animals. Their bodies are small on the top and large and heavy on the bottom. A typical macropod has short, thin front legs with small, hand-like paws. Its hind legs, on the other hand, are large and powerful. And of course, it has those enormous feet.

Each of a macropod's hind feet has one very long middle toe and three shorter toes. Two of the shorter toes are joined together and are used as a "comb" in grooming fur. Kangaroos hop mainly on their long, strong middle toes.

All kangaroos hop, but the champion hoppers belong to the macropod family. A large macropod such as a red kangaroo has a "cruising speed" of 15 to 20 miles per hour (about 24–32 km/hr).

Like all macropods, this red kangaroo has short front legs and large, powerful hind legs.

13

Moving at cruising speed, kangaroos actually use less energy in hopping on two legs than an animal does running on four legs. The marsupials have large **tendons** made of elastic tissue in their legs, lower backs, and tails. These tendons store energy in something like the way that the spring of a pogo stick does. As a kangaroo hops, energy continues to be built up in the tendons and then released. The animal needs very little additional energy to keep moving.

A western gray kangaroo hopping at cruising speed

When hopping, a kangaroo always moves both hind legs together. The hind legs move independently when the marsupial swims.

To increase its speed, a kangaroo usually makes each hop longer rather than hopping more times. Red kangaroos have been known to cover 35 feet (10.7 m) in one hop and to reach speeds of 40 miles per hour (64 km/hr). But they can move this fast for only a short time. At such high speeds, kangaroos use up more energy than is stored in their tendons.

Hopping is also not very practical at low speeds. When a kangaroo has to move slowly, while feeding on grass, for example, it uses something called a "crawl-walk." With its front feet and the bottom part of its tail on the ground, it swings both hind legs forward at the same time.

Some macropods put hopping to special uses. Rock wallabies (below) spend most of their time on rocky ledges and cliffs. These small marsupials can make jumps of more than 20 feet (6 m), landing with the skill of mountain goats. A rock wallaby's feet have rough, bumpy skin on the soles that provides a good grip. When jumping, a rock wallaby extends its long, slender tail out behind for extra balance.

Rock wallabies live in warm, dry regions in many parts of Australia. They hide in caves and crevices during the day and come out during the night to eat grass and leaves.

Tree kangaroos (above) do their jumping among the branches of trees. These unusual macropods have longer front legs and shorter hind legs than other kangaroos. Their broad hind feet have roughened pads used for gripping. Sharp claws on their front feet help them to cling to tree trunks and branches.

In their treetop homes, tree kangaroos walk along branches on all four feet. They leap from one tree to another, sometimes jumping as far as 30 feet (9 m). On the ground, tree kangaroos hop on their hind feet, just like their relatives.

Two kinds of tree kangaroos live in the rain forests of Australia, while seven other species are found in New Guinea and a few other islands. All snooze the day away while perched on branches and move around munching leaves and fruit at night.

EATING

To supply energy for hopping and their other activities, kangaroos need food. The diet of some rat kangaroos—for example, the potoroo—includes insects and worms, but macropods are **herbivores** (ERB-ih-vors). They eat only green plants.

Large macropods such as the red kangaroo and the two varieties of gray kangaroo feed mainly on grass. They graze in much the same way as antelopes and sheep do, moving slowly along with heads down, biting off mouthfuls of grass. Wallaroos and the larger wallabies also eat in this way.

Other wallabies have a more varied diet. They eat leaves and other plant parts, as well as grass. Sometimes they use their small front paws to hold food while eating.

The diet of this red-necked wallaby includes tree bark and leaves as well as grass.

Red kangaroo grazing on dry grass

The plants that many macropods eat are tough and hard to chew, but the marsupials are specially equipped to handle this diet. Grazing kangaroos have thin, sharp front teeth suited for feeding on short, coarse grass. Large molars in the back of the kangaroos' mouths chop up and grind tough plant parts.

As a kangaroo's molars wear out, they move slowly forward to the front of the jaw and fall out. New molars move in from the back to take their place. Most kangaroos get 16 new molars during their lifetimes.

Plant material, especially grass, does not make a nourishing diet. Kangaroos have to eat a lot to satisfy their needs. Their method of digestion also helps to make their food more nourishing. Like other plant-eating animals such as cattle and sheep, kangaroos have tiny organisms living in their digestive systems. These organisms break down plant material by a process called **fermentation.**

Western gray kangaroos feed on grass in the forested regions where they make their homes.

Many kangaroos can survive on the moisture contained in plants, but like this female red kangaroo, they drink water when it is available.

DRINKING

For many kangaroos, plants provide not only nourishment but also moisture. Their bodies make such good use of the moisture in their diet that they seldom need to drink water. This is particularly true of macropods that live in very dry areas, such as the red kangaroo. Other species living in wetter regions—for example, the gray kangaroo—drink more often.

Tammar wallabies can drink salty seawater. These macropods live on islands where there is little freshwater.

KEEPING COOL

Because so many kangaroos live in hot climates, they are experts at keeping cool. One method they use is limiting their activities to the cooler hours of the night. Rock wallabies spend the day hidden in caves and rock crevices. Gray kangaroos stay in the shade of the forest, venturing out on the plains at night to feed.

Red kangaroos live in areas where there are few trees or rocks to provide shade. These big macropods sometimes beat the heat by digging shallow holes to reach the cooler layers of soil beneath the surface. Then they flop down for a nap.

When kangaroos can't find a shady spot, they use a special method of keeping cool. They lick their front legs, spreading them with a heavy coat of saliva. How does this make them cooler? A kangaroo's front legs have many small blood vessels close to the surface. The evaporation of the saliva cools the blood as it passes through these vessels, lowering the animal's body heat.

LIVING TOGETHER

On the Australian grasslands, large numbers of kangaroos can often be seen grazing together or sleeping in the shade. Are these animals part of a group? Or do they just happen to be in the same place at the same time?

Scientists believe that at least some kangaroos do form groups. Most small potoroid kangaroos live alone, but many macropods live with others of their kind. Researchers are studying them to find out just what their social lives are like.

Western gray kangaroos are social animals that form large groups.

Although seen alone in this picture, a whiptail wallaby usually lives with others of its kind.

Antilopine wallaroos and gray and red kangaroos seem to be the most social members of the macropod family. These species live together in loose groups that may be as small as two or three members or as large as one hundred.

Scientists use the term **mob** for larger groups of kangaroos. The members of a mob share the same **home range,** the area in which they find food and shelter. Mobs include adult males and females, as well as young kangaroos of various ages.

In most mobs, some animals are **dominant** over the others. These individuals are large and strong or have other traits that make them superior to fellow mob members.

Male kangaroos sometimes fight to establish dominance. Two opponents stand tall on their hind legs, supporting themselves with their tails. They paw and strike at each other with their front legs, heads tipped back to avoid sharp claws. Sometimes one kangaroo will balance on his tail and kick his opponent in the stomach with both hind legs.

By means of such battles, male kangaroos work out their positions in the group. Dominant males are at the top of the heap. They take the best grazing spots and the shadiest places to sleep. When mating time comes, they have a chance to mate with more females than other males in the group.

This female red-necked wallaby is an albino, with pure white fur and pink eyes. The female mated with a normal red-necked male, and the baby, or joey, in her pouch has the usual brown coloring of the species.

An adult female kangaroo almost always has one baby in her pouch and another at her side (right).

HAVING YOUNG

The only role that male kangaroos play in reproduction is mating. But females devote almost their whole lives to producing young. In many species, an adult female always has one **joey,** or baby, in her pouch, an older joey at her side, and a third young one developing inside her body.

A young kangaroo stays inside its mother's body for a very short time. The average period is about 32 days, but in some species it is only 21 days. For comparison, a human baby develops inside its mother for 9 months (about 270 days), and a baby elephant stays inside its mother for 18 months.

This difference in early development is what separates marsupials from other kinds of mammals. Humans and elephants belong to a group known as **placental** (pluh-SENT-uhl) **mammals.** A baby placental mammal goes through its early growth inside its mother's body, where it is nourished by an organ called the placenta. For a young marsupial, the longest period of development takes place not inside the mother's body, but in her pouch.

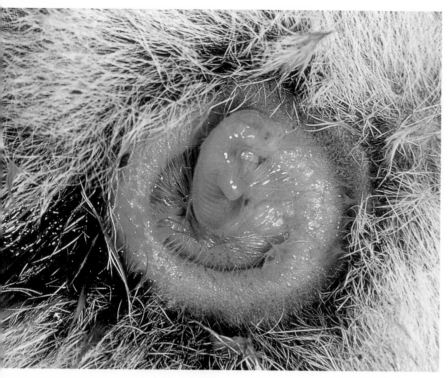

Left: *A young Tammar wallaby emerging from its mother's body*
Below: *At two days old, the tiny wallaby is firmly attached to a nipple in the mother's pouch.*

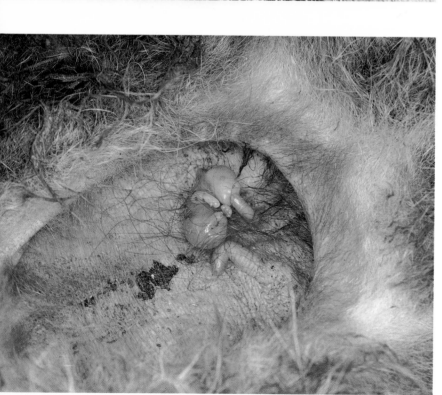

One or two days before a female kangaroo gives birth, she gets ready by cleaning out her pouch. Putting her head inside, she gives the lining of the pouch a thorough licking. When it's time for the birth, the female leans back against a tree or rock, with her hind legs and tail extended in front of her.

The baby that emerges from her body is about the size of a kidney bean. It is hairless and cannot see or hear. Its skeleton is made up not of hard bone but of a soft material called **cartilage** (KAR-tih-lij). The joey's hind legs are just beginning to take shape, but its front legs are well developed, and so is its sense of smell.

30

Using its strong front legs, the joey climbs up through the fur on its mother's stomach to the opening of her pouch. The trip is not long, but it is full of danger. If the baby falls off, it will not be able to survive. The mother kangaroo can give no help to her youngster during this dangerous journey.

Once inside the pouch, the joey's sense of smell guides it to one of its mother's four nipples. The tiny baby grabs on, and the nipple expands inside its mouth. The joey will spend the next 4 months firmly attached to its mother's nipple, drinking milk and growing.

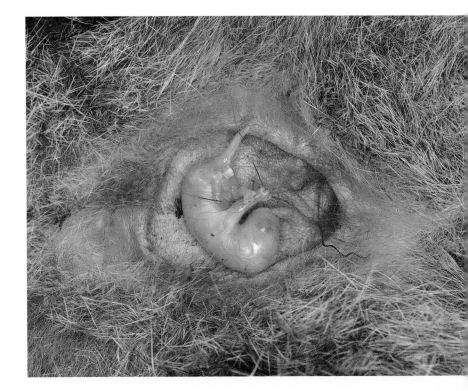

A Tammar wallaby at 3 weeks (top) and *12 weeks (right). During this period, the joey's hind legs develop, and long claws form on all four feet.*

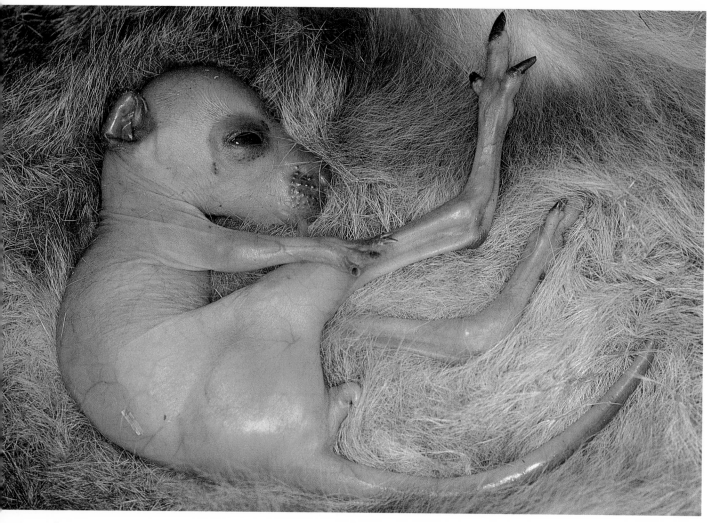

Above: *A Tammar wallaby at 17 weeks.* **Opposite:** *This young red kangaroo is about 6 months old and ready to leave the pouch for short periods of time.*

A kangaroo joey develops slowly during the first months of its life. Its hind legs take shape, and its fur begins to grow. Its skeleton hardens. In many species, the joey's eyes do not open until it is around 4 months old (above). By this time, it is starting to move inside the pouch. Soon the joey will put its head out to take its first look at the world.

After 4 months, the joey begins to develop more rapidly. Its mother's milk has changed in its makeup to include more fat and other nutrients that the joey needs. On this nourishing diet, the joey completes its growth.

A red kangaroo joey (shown on these pages) first leaves the pouch when it is about 6 months old. It may spend only a few minutes outside before hurrying back. The mother kangaroo bends down to make it easier for her baby to get back into the pouch. The joey jumps in head first, kicking off with its strong hind legs. It does a somersault inside the pouch to get in an upright position.

As the red kangaroo joey gets older, it spends more and more time outside its mother's pouch, returning only to nurse or to sleep. By the time it is 8 months old, it is too big to fit in the pouch.

A female red kangaroo and her joey relaxing in the sun. Although almost grown, the joey still spends some time in its mother's pouch.

At 8 months old, a red kangaroo joey is eating grass, but it will continue to nurse for several more months. It sticks its head in the pouch to drink from the same nipple it used earlier. By this time, there is usually a new joey attached to another nipple.

Amazingly, the female kangaroo's body produces a different kind of milk from each nipple. The content of the milk is perfectly suited to each youngster's needs and stage of development.

A joey that has left the pouch is often called a **young-at-foot** because it stays so close to its mother. The youngster follows her around, feeding and resting at her side. If danger threatens, the mother warns her joey by stamping her foot. Together they hop away from the threat.

When red kangaroo joeys stop nursing at around 1 year old, they gradually become more independent and learn to live on their own. At the age of 18 months, they are full grown. Young female kangaroos often stay in the same mob as their mothers, while males usually join other groups.

36

Australian Aborigines often pictured kangaroos in their art. This is a bark painting showing two kangaroos, a lizard, and a canoe.

KANGAROOS PAST, PRESENT, AND FUTURE

Kangaroos have lived in Australia for thousands of years. In ancient times, macropods more than 7 feet tall roamed the Australian plains. The Aborigines hunted these large kangaroos and other marsupials for food. Kangaroos also played an important role in the stories and legends that native people told about the natural world.

Europeans first reached Australia during the 1600s, and they were amazed by the continent's animal life. In 1629, a Dutch explorer saw a female wallaby with a joey nursing in her pouch. After taking a close look, he decided that the baby must have grown directly out of the female's nipple.

When Europeans began to settle in Australia during the 1700s, they became more familiar with the continent's marsupial population. Like the native people, settlers hunted kangaroos for food.

During the 1800s, European settlers in Australia hunted large macropods like these red kangaroos for sport, chasing them on horseback with the help of hunting dogs.

As more and more Europeans made new homes in Australia, attitudes toward kangaroos began to change. The continent's dry grasslands seemed ideal for raising cattle and sheep, but these were the same areas where thousands of kangaroos lived. During the late 1800s, sheep farming became an important industry in Australia, and kangaroos began to be seen as pests, taking precious grass and water needed by sheep.

More than 100 years later, sheep are still important in Australia, and kangaroos are still considered a problem. In some areas, kangaroo populations have increased dramatically because sheep farming has made more grazing land available. As many as 20 million red and gray kangaroos roam the Australian grasslands.

Most researchers claim that kangaroos do not usually compete with domesticated animals for food and water. But during dry periods, there is often not enough grass for both sheep and kangaroos.

To help sheep farmers, the Australian government allows some kangaroos to be killed each year. Government officials establish quotas in different areas based on local kangaroo populations.

Under the quota system, about 3 to 5 million red and gray kangaroos are killed annually. Professional hunters are given licenses to shoot the animals with powerful rifles. The meat is sold to pet-food companies, and the hides are used to make leather.

This male and female with a joey are among the millions of red kangaroos that live in modern Australia. The large macropods sometimes compete with domesticated animals for food and water.

The Parma wallaby is a rare species that was once thought to be extinct. In the 1960s, a small number of these marsupials were rediscovered in eastern Australia.

Some Australians, as well as people in other parts of the world, are not happy with this solution to the kangaroo "problem." They want to find some other way to deal with this conflict between animals and people. One suggestion is that Australian sheep farmers should raise fewer sheep and instead try kangaroo ranching.

Under this plan, some of the kangaroos roaming the open range would be killed and their meat sold as human food. People who support this idea say that kangaroos cause less harm to the environment than sheep. If farmers could make a living by rounding up and selling kangaroos, it might be a good thing for everyone, even the marsupials.

While overpopulation seems to be a problem for some kangaroo species, other species are in danger of extinction. Many smaller members of the macropod family are in trouble, and some species have already disappeared. For example, several kinds of wallabies, including the toolache wallaby, have not been seen for many years.

In some parts of Australia, endangered kangaroos are losing their living space because of humans. The forests where tree kangaroos live are being cut down for lumber, and the marsupials have been forced into smaller and smaller areas.

This young Bennett's wallaby has white fur that will change to gray brown as the animal gets older. Large numbers of Bennett's wallabies live on the island of Tasmania, which is a part of Australia. The wallabies are considered pests because they feed on young trees being grown for timber. To prevent this damage, the Tasmanian government has allowed Bennett's wallabies to be killed with poison.

As part of a research project, this kangaroo has been fitted with a radio collar. Signals sent out by the collar enable scientists to track the kangaroo and to learn more about its behavior. Such information may be useful in protecting Australia's kangaroo population.

Other kangaroos are being killed by wild animals brought from Europe. European foxes attack rock wallabies and other small macropods. Even domestic cats that have become wild are a threat to the smallest members of the macropod family.

To protect the small marsupials, the Australian government is trying to reduce the population of foxes and other non-native wild animals. Other conservation efforts include the establishing of parks and nature reserves in areas where endangered kangaroos live. In these places, marsupials can find refuge from humans and their destructive activities.

GLOSSARY

cartilage: flexible tissue that makes up the skeleton of a young marsupial. As the baby grows, the cartilage hardens into bone.

dominant: taking first place in a group of animals. A dominant male kangaroo usually mates with more females than other males in the group.

families: smaller groups that make up a scientific order. Kangaroos belong to two families—Potoroidae and Macropodidae.

fermentation: the process by which living organisms such as bacteria break down plant material. Like cattle and other plant-eating animals, kangaroos have these organisms in their digestive systems.

herbivores: animals that eat only plants

home range: the area where an animal lives and finds food. Kangaroos in groups share the same home range.

joey: a baby kangaroo

macropods: "big-foot" kangaroos, members of the family Macropodidae

mammals: animals that feed their young with milk produced by mammary glands. Kangaroos are marsupial mammals; humans are placental mammals.

marsupial: an animal whose young are born in a very early stage of development. A marsupial baby finishes its growth in a pouch on the outside of its mother's body.

mob: a group of kangaroos living together

order: a large group within the system of scientific classification. Kangaroos belong to the order Marsupialia. (See also families; species)

placental mammals: animals whose unborn young are nourished by an organ called the placenta. Placental mammals go through their early development inside their mothers' bodies.

potoroids: rat kangaroos, members of the family Potoroidae

species: a group of animals with many characteristics in common

tendons: bands of elastic fibrous tissue in a kangaroo's legs, back, and tail. When the animal hops, energy is stored in the tendons.

young-at-foot: a young kangaroo that has left the pouch but stays close to its mother for protection

INDEX

ABOUT THE AUTHOR

Denise Burt is an author and publisher, with a very strong interest in the flora and fauna of her Australian homeland. She has had numerous children's books published, as well as educational material for classroom use. She lives with her husband in suburban Melbourne but plans eventually to live in the country.

ABOUT THE PHOTOGRAPHER

Neil McLeod is a man of many interests. He is a nature photographer, painter, publisher, naturalist, and adventurer. He travels a lot in outback Australia, living and working with Aborigines to observe their customs and to add to his already extensive knowledge. He has published over thirty books about Australia and its native animals.